The Union in Crisis
Chapter Resource File with Answer Key

HOLT

American Anthem
Modern American History

HOLT, RINEHART AND WINSTON

A Harcourt Education Company

Orlando • **Austin** • New York • San Diego • London

Contents

The Union in Crisis

Vocabulary Builder

Section 1

Compromise of 1850	Fugitive Slave Act	Kansas-Nebraska Act
Lincoln-Douglas debates	popular sovereignty	context
Confederate States of America		

DIRECTIONS Look at each set of four terms. On the line provided, write the letter of the term that does not relate to the others.

_____ 1. a. John Brown's raid
b. popular sovereignty
c. Sack of Lawrence
d. Kansas-Nebraska Act

_____ 2. a. South Carolina
b. Confederate States of America
c. Jefferson Davis
d. abolition

_____ 3. a. secession
b. Lincoln-Douglas debates
c. Freeport Doctrine
d. popular sovereignty

_____ 4. a. Fugitive Slave Act
b. California
c. runaway slaves
d. controversial

DIRECTIONS Answer each question by writing a sentence that contains at least one word from the word bank.

5. What plan was proposed by Senator Henry Clay to preserve the balance of power in Congress?

____

____

____

6. What was the name of the association created by the seven seceded states, and how did it protect the institution of slavery?

____

____

____

7. What act made Abraham Lincoln feel "thunderstruck and stunned," and how did he react to that act?

____

____

____

The Union in Crisis   Vocabulary Builder

Section 2

Battle of Antietam	Battle of Bull Run	Battle of Chancellorsville
Battle of Gettysburg	Battle of Shiloh	Emancipation Proclamation
Fort Sumter	Thirteenth Amendment	

DIRECTIONS Read each sentence and fill in the blank with the word in the word pair that best completes the sentence.

1. In the ______________________, General George Pickett's men attacked the center of the Union lines on Cemetery Ridge. **(Battle of Antietam/Battle of Gettysburg)**

2. The ______________________ freed enslaved people in all areas that were in rebellion against the United States.
(Emancipation Proclamation/Thirteenth Amendment)

3. During the ______________________, not only Union troops but also onlookers fled the battlefield. **(Battle of Chancellorsville/Battle of Bull Run)**

4. Confederate troops surprised Union troops at dinnertime during the

______________________. **(Battle of Shiloh/Battle of Chancellorsville)**

5. The ______________________ was considered a Union victory, but only because General Robert E. Lee's invasion was stopped.
(Battle of Antietam/Battle of Shiloh)

6. After Abraham Lincoln defeated George McClellan in the 1864 presidential election,

Congress passed the ______________________, which ended slavery in the United

States. **(Thirteenth Amendment/Emancipation Proclamation)**

7. Northern hopes that the South's rebellion would collapse on its own ended after the

______________________. **(Battle of Bull Run/Battle of Shiloh)**

DIRECTIONS Choose five of the vocabulary words from the word list. On a separate sheet of paper use these words to write a letter that relates to the section.

The Union in Crisis   Vocabulary Builder

Section 3

carpetbagger	Civil Rights Act of 1866	contract
Fifteenth Amendment	Fourteenth Amendment	Ku Klux Klan
Liberal Republicans	prejudice	Reconstruction
scalawag	sharecropping	tenant farming
utilize		

DIRECTIONS Choose five of the vocabulary words from the word list.
Use these words to write a summary of what you learned in the section.

____

____

____

____

____

____

DIRECTIONS Read each sentence and fill in the blank with the word in
the word pair that best completes the sentence.

1. The _____________________ required states to grant citizenship to "all persons
   born or naturalized in the United States" and promised "equal protection of the laws."
   (Fourteenth Amendment/Fifteenth Amendment)

2. The _____________________ terrorized African Americans and whites who
   supported their rights. **(Ku Klux Klan/Liberal Republicans)**

3. Northerners who came south during Reconstruction to take part in the region's

   political and economic rebirth were known as _____________________.

   (scalawags/carpetbaggers)

4. In the system known as _____________________, freedmen received a portion of
   their employer's crop instead of wages. **(tenant farming/sharecropping)**

5. The _____________________ protected the voting rights of African American
   males. **(Civil Rights Act of 1866/Fifteenth Amendment)**

6. Conditions in the South strengthened the _____________________, who helped
   Democrats regain power in Congress in 1872. **(Liberal Republicans/scalawags)**

Harriet Beecher Stowe

1811–1896

WHY SHE MADE HISTORY An accomplished author, Harriet Beecher Stowe is best known for her novel *Uncle Tom's Cabin*. Her story exposed the brutality of slavery and increased tensions between the North and South prior to the Civil War.

The Art Archive/Culver Pictures

As you read the biography below, think about the impact *Uncle Tom's Cabin* had on the Civil War. Why do you think the book stirred such strong emotional responses?

In the years prior to the Civil War, people in the North and South lived very different lives. Ultimately, the northern and southern states were divided by their positions on the issue of slavery. Author Harriet Beecher Stowe's novel *Uncle Tom's Cabin* increased the tensions that led to war.

Harriet Beecher was born in 1811 in Litchfield, Connecticut. She was the daughter of a prominent Congregationalist minister and a member of a highly intellectual family. Harriet attended the Litchfield Female Academy, and later the Hartford Female Seminary in Hartford, Connecticut, which was run by her sister. Beecher taught at the seminary after graduating.

In 1832 Beecher and her father and sister moved to Cincinnati, Ohio. Her father became president of the Lane Theological Seminary, and Beecher began teaching at another school started by her sister. It was in Cincinnati that she met and married clergyman and professor Calvin Ellis Stowe. She also began writing stories for local journals.

For 18 years, Harriet Beecher Stowe lived in Cincinnati, just across the river from a slave-holding community. She met many fugitive slaves there, and learned about life in the South. In 1849 her 18-month-old son Samuel Charles died from cholera. Stowe said the experience taught her what a slave mother must go through when her child was taken from her.

In 1850 the Fugitive Slave Act was passed. The law was designed to encourage people in northern states to help capture and return runaway slaves. That same year, Stowe began writing *Uncle Tom's Cabin*. She published sections of the book in an antislavery newspaper. The book tells the story of a fictional slave, Tom. Tom is a faithful slave who is sold, and resold, and eventually dies from a beating at the hands of his owner.

The Union in Crisis   Biography

When *Uncle Tom's Cabin* was published in book form, it sold over 300,000 copies in its first year. It was also turned into a stage play. The book was a hit with abolitionists, but it was hated by southerners who supported slavery. The story stirred antislavery and pro-slavery sentiments, and increased tensions between the North and South prior to the Civil War. In fact, upon meeting Stowe, President Abraham Lincoln reportedly said: "So you're the little woman who wrote the book that started this great war."

Uncle Tom's Cabin was the focus of criticism and controversy. In response, Stowe published *A Key to Uncle Tom's Cabin* in 1853. This book tried to provide answers to the questions raised by critics. Stowe also began traveling in Europe and speaking to antislavery organizations.

The story of Uncle Tom was not Stowe's only attempt to communicate her position on a social issue through fiction. She continued to write, much as her father preached, to address social issues. She wrote about the role of women, reform, Christianity, and domestic politics.

Stowe published her last book in 1878. It was a fictionalized memoir of her childhood. By then many critics dismissed her writing as melodramatic and her characters as stereotypes. She died in Hartford in 1896.

During the women's movement of the 1970s, Stowe's writings saw a resurgence in popularity, and her role in speaking out for the oppressed was again recognized. *Uncle Tom's Cabin* continues to be read and discussed for the role it played in bringing the nation's attention to the realities of slavery.

WHAT DID YOU LEARN?

1. **Identify** Harriet Beecher Stowe was born into a prominent family. What did her father do?

   ____

   ____

2. **Summarize** What did *Uncle Tom's Cabin* come to symbolize?

   ____

   ____

ACTIVITY

Uncle Tom's Cabin has been presented as a stage play. With a group of students, select a scene from the play or the book to present to the class. Discuss the scenes presented. What did the scenes teach you about slavery and America in the years prior to the Civil War?

Stonewall Jackson

1824–1863

WHY HE MADE HISTORY The military skill and heroism of Stonewall Jackson made him a serious opponent to Union forces and an asset to Confederate commander Robert E. Lee.

As you read the biography below, look for examples of Jackson's military skill. What role did he play in the outcome of the war?

At a time when the South was feeling the weight of northern military force, Thomas Jonathan "Stonewall" Jackson emerged as a hero for the southern people. Under the command of Gen. Robert E. Lee, Jackson made a name for himself on the battlefield. Even when his troops were badly outnumbered by the enemy, he was able to maintain command and hold a position. It was nearly impossible for northern forces to get past him.

Orphaned at an early age, Jackson was raised by relatives. He showed little evidence of future greatness. Although his educational and social skills were poor, he gained admission to the U.S. Military Academy at West Point. He studied with determination to improve his class rank and graduated with a respectable record.

After graduation, Jackson fought in the Mexican American War, where his bravery and resourcefulness in battle earned him promotions. A few years later he resigned his post with the army and went on to teach for 10 years at the Virginia Military Institute (VMI). He was not highly regarded by students there and was often the subject of their pranks.

When the Civil War broke out, Jackson volunteered for the Confederate Army and led a group of VMI cadets to Richmond where they drilled new recruits. A few months later Jackson was promoted to brigadier general.

During the First Battle of Manassas, another general, trying to rally his troops, pointed to Jackson standing atop a hill. The general said, "Look, men! There stands Jackson like a stone wall! Rally behind the Virginians!" The Confederates won the battle and Jackson earned the nickname "Stonewall."

Jackson emerged as a military genius known for staging surprise attacks. He would ride on his favorite horse, Little Sorrell, at the head of his troops. He guided his troops around enemy lines, identified the weakest spot, and attacked quickly and unexpectedly.

The Union in Crisis   Biography

Jackson was the most able of Robert E. Lee's generals and was credited with many victories in the early years of the war. These victories kept Confederate hopes and spirits alive.

Stonewall Jackson's glory was short-lived. He died after a successful attack against Union forces at Chancellorsville. His own men failed to recognize him and shot him as he rode into camp. Jackson was taken to a field hospital, and his left arm was amputated. He seemed to be recovering when he came down with pneumonia. Without the benefit of modern-day penicillin or antibiotics, Jackson died of the disease.

At his request, Jackson was buried at VMI. The cemetery there was renamed the Stonewall Jackson Cemetery. Because Jackson was said to love lemons, visitors often leave baskets of lemons at his grave. Little Sorrell, his horse, lived until 1886 at VMI, grazing on the school's parade grounds under the care of VMI cadets.

WHAT DID YOU LEARN?

1. **Recall** Why was Stonewall Jackson considered the most able of Lee's generals?

____

____

2. **Make Judgments** Select two words that you feel describe Stonewall Jackson. Explain your choices.

____

____

ACTIVITY

With a small group of classmates, read more about the military strategies of Stonewall Jackson. Work together to create a map of one of Jackson's military campaigns. Include a description of the battle with your map, and present your map to the class.

Sojourner Truth

c. 1797–1883

WHY SHE MADE HISTORY An African American evangelist and reformer, Sojourner Truth supported women's rights and the abolition of slavery.

As you read the biography below, think about *Sojourner Truth's beliefs. Why did she speak out against slavery and for women's rights? Why do you think people listened to what she had to say?*

In the years prior to the Civil War, many people spoke out against slavery. One of the most outspoken supporters of abolition was Sojourner Truth, a former slave. Truth gained her freedom when the state of New York declared slavery illegal. She spent her life working to help slaves.

The daughter of slaves, Sojourner Truth was born Isabella Baumfree in Ulster, New York, around 1797. Her first language was Dutch because her parents spoke this language. She spent much of her childhood living with different slave owners. The most notable was the Dumont family.

About 1815 Baumfree married a fellow slave named Thomas. They had five children. The couple separated some time after 1827, the year that slavery was declared illegal in New York. When a member of the Dumont family illegally sold one of her sons into slavery, Baumfree sued in court and won his return. Around the same time, Baumfree became a born-again Christian. She moved to New York City and supported herself by working as a housekeeper.

Growing up, Baumfree had many visions. She believed these visions came from God. Baumfree was active in the Methodist Church, and became a missionary preaching in the streets.

In 1843 Baumfree began using the name Sojourner Truth, which roughly means someone who travels from place to place telling the truth. She believed she had been called upon by the Holy Spirit to spread the word of God. She traveled to many cities and towns, and often preached to large crowds. She also became an outspoken advocate of women's rights and abolition. She ultimately moved to a utopian community in Northampton, Massachusetts, and became involved in antislavery meetings there.

Her autobiography, *The Narrative of Sojourner Truth*, was published in 1850. Truth supported herself with money from book sales and continued

The Union in Crisis

Biography

to travel the country preaching and advocating for women's rights. She settled in Battle Creek, Michigan, in the 1850s.

During the Civil War, Sojourner Truth helped gather supplies for African American volunteer regiments. In 1864 she went to Washington to help integrate streetcars. She also visited President Abraham Lincoln in the White House. After the war, Truth suggested creating a state for former slaves in the West and helped counsel former enslaved African Americans.

Sojourner Truth retired in 1875 and remained in Battle Creek until her death eight years later.

WHAT DID YOU LEARN?

1. **Describe** How did Sojourner Truth help the Civil War effort?

____

____

2. **Analyze** Why did Sojourner Truth preach to people everywhere?

____

____

ACTIVITY

Sojourner Truth advocated for women's rights and the abolition of slavery. How do you view Sojourner Truth? Write a short essay that explains what Sojourner Truth's life and legacy mean to you.

Shiloh

Shelby Foote

ABOUT THE READING In *Shiloh*, novelist and Civil War historian Shelby Foote tells the story of the battle at Shiloh (fought in April 1862) through the eyes of the Union and Confederate soldiers who were there. The book begins with Lieutenant Palmer Metcalfe, age 19, marching to the battle with the Confederate Army; it ends with the same soldier coming away after his leader has died. The following excerpt is from the final chapter as Palmer remembers the last time he saw General Johnston alive.

As you read the passage below, watch for actions that might be called heroic or brave. The following words might be new to you: **moribund**, **romanticism**, **chivalry**. *You may want to use a dictionary to look them up.*

I found my mind went idle and I saw again General Johnston the way I had seen him at two oclock Sunday afternoon, the last time I saw him alive.

One of Breckinridge's brigades had recoiled from a charge against a ridge in the Hornets Nest and the officers were having trouble getting them back into line to go forward again; they didn't want any more of it right then. General Johnston watched this for a while, then rode out front. He had taken his hat off, holding it with his left hand against his thigh, and in his right hand he held the small tin cup he had picked up in a captured camp earlier in the day. As he passed down the line he leaned sideways in the saddle and touched the points of the bayonets with the cup. It made a little clink each time.

"These must do the work," he said.

When the line had formed, he rode front and center and turned his horse—Fire-eater, a thoroughbred bay—toward the crest where the Union troops were waiting.

"I will lead you!" he cried.

The men sent up a shout. General Johnston set spurs in his horse and the brigade went forward, cheering, at a run. Charging through the thickest fire I ever saw, they took the crest, halted to re-form, and stood there waving their flags and yelling so loud that the leaves on the trees seemed to tremble. The general came riding back with a smile on his face, teeth flashing beneath his mustache. His battle blood was up; his eyes had a shine like bright glass. Fire-eater was hit in four places. There were rips and tears in the general's uniform and his left bootsole had been cut nearly in half by a minie ball. He shook his foot so the dangling leather flapped.

"They didn't trip me up that time!" he said, laughing.

The Union in Crisis   Literature

This was the charge that began to break the Hornets Nest. I was sent with a message for Beauregard [another general] on the other flank, telling him we were moving forward again, and when I came back General Johnston's body was already stretched out for removal from the field. They told me how he died—from a wound in the right leg, a hurt so slight that anyone with simple knowledge of tourniquets could have saved him. Doctor Yandell, his surgeon, had been with him all through the battle, but shortly before the final attack near the peach orchard, the general ordered him to establish an aid station for a group of Federal wounded he saw at one point on the field. When the doctor protested, General Johnston cut him off.

"These men were our enemies a moment ago," he said. "They are our prisoners now. Take care of them."

When I heard this, that the general had died because of his consideration for men who a short time before had been shooting at him and doing all in their power to wreck his cause, I remembered what my father had said about the South bearing within itself the seeds of defeat, the Confederacy being conceived already **moribund**. We were sick from an old malady, he said: incurable **romanticism** and misplaced **chivalry**, too much Walter Scott and Dumas read too seriously. We were in love with the past, he said; in love with death.

He enjoyed posing as a realist and straight thinker—war was more shovelry than chivalry, he said—but he was a highly romantic figure of a man himself and he knew it, he with his creased forehead and his tales of the war in Texas, with his empty sleeve and his midnight drinking beneath the portrait of his wife in the big empty house in New Orleans. He talked that way because of some urge for self-destruction, some compulsion to hate what he had become: an old man with a tragic life, who sent his son off to a war he was too maimed to take part in himself. It was regret. It was regret of a particular regional form.

ANALYZING LITERATURE

1. **Main Idea** What do you know about General Johnston after reading this excerpt?

____

____

2. **Critical Thinking: Inference** What do you think Palmer's father means by "romanticism and misplaced chivalry"? Give examples from the excerpt.

____

____

Southern and Northern Reactions to the Civil War

ABOUT THE SOURCE When Abraham Lincoln assumed the presidency in March 1861, the seven states of the Deep South had already seceded. Confederate forces in these states seized federal forts. Only Fort Sumter, in South Carolina's Charleston harbor, remained in Union hands. Its commander refused to surrender. On April 12, 1861, Confederate guns fired on the fort, marking the start of the Civil War. In the passages below, two women describe how southerners and northerners reacted to the outbreak of war.

As you read note how the perspectives of the two women differ. The following words may be new to you: **solaced**, **insurrection**, **furrow**, **rendezvous**, **festooned**. *You may want to use a dictionary to look them up.*

Mary Boykin Chesnut
Chesnut was in Charleston, South Carolina as the Confederates prepared to attack Fort Sumter. She wrote the following in her journal on April 7, 1861.

The air is too full of war news. And we are all so restless. News so warlike I quake. My husband speaks of joining the artillery . . . Now the agony was so stifling—I could hardly see or hear . . . And I crept silently to my room, where I sat down to a good cry. Mrs. Wigfall came in, and we had it out on the subject of civil war. We **solaced** ourselves with dwelling on all its known horrors, and then we added what we had a right to expect, with Yankees in front and negroes in the rear.

"The slave-owners must expect a servile **insurrection**, of course," said Mrs. Wigfall, to make sure that we were unhappy enough. Suddenly, loud shouting was heard. We ran out. Cannon after cannon roared . . . Governor Means rushed out of his room . . . and begged us to be calm.

"Governor Pickens has ordered . . . seven cannon to be fired as a signal to the Seventh Regiment . . ."

No sleep for anybody last night. The streets were alive with soldiers, men shouting, marching, singing.

Source: *Mary Chesnut's Civil War*, edited by C. Vann Woodward

WHAT DID YOU LEARN?

1. How did Chesnut feel about the outbreak of war? Why did she feel this way?

____

____

The Union in Crisis

Primary Source

Mary Ashton Livermore
Livermore was in Boston when Fort Sumter surrendered to the South. Writing years later, she recalled how New Englanders reacted to the start of the war.

Everywhere the drum and fife thrilled the air with their stirring call. Recruiting offices were opened in every city, town, and village. No stimulus was needed. The plough was left in the **furrow**; the carpenter turned from the bench; the student closed his books; the clerk abandoned the counting-room; the lawyer forsook his clients; and even the clergymen exchanged his pulpit for the camp and the tented field, preaching no longer the gospel of peace, but the duty of war. Hastily formed companies marched to camps of **rendezvous**, the sunlight flashing from gun-barrel and bayonet, and the streets echoing the measured tread of soldiers. Flags floated from the roofs of houses, were flung to the breeze from chambers of commerce and boards of trade, spanned the surging streets, decorated the private parlor, glorified the school-room, **festooned** the church walls and pulpit, and blossomed everywhere. All normal habits of life were suspended, and business and pleasure alike were forgotten.

Source: Mary A. Livermore, *My Story of the War: A Woman's Narrative, 1887*

WHAT DID YOU LEARN?

1. How did people in New England respond to the outbreak of civil war?

____

____

____

MAKE A COMPARISON

1. According to these sources how did the southern reaction to the outbreak of war compare to the northern reaction to the outbreak of war?

____

____

____

2. How do the above passages differ from each other? Why do you think they are different?

____

____

____

Report of the South Carolina Freedmen's Bureau

ABOUT THE SOURCE In March 1865 Congress created the Bureau of Refugees, Freedmen, and Abandoned Lands. Called the Freedmen's Bureau, the agency's purpose was to help newly-freed slaves adjust to life in the post-Civil War South. President Andrew Johnson objected to the Bureau's policy of giving plots of land to freedmen. Nonetheless, in July 1866 Congress renewed the Bureau and expanded its size. The passage below is from a report to Congress by the Assistant Commissioner of the Freedmen's Bureau in South Carolina. The report was dated November 1, 1866.

As you read note the challenges the Freedmen's Bureau faced in South Carolina. The following words may be new to you: **ferreting, perpetrators, collusion, infirm, avidity.** *You may want to use a dictionary to look them up.*

I found the freed people in a most wretched condition from want of clothing and food. They were treated generally in a most cruel and, in many instances, a most barbarous manner by their former masters, who seemed to be doubly bitter because they could no longer hold them as slaves. Outrages, such as whipping, tying up by the thumbs, and shooting, were of daily occurrence, and the force of troops in the State was totally inadequate to meet the demands made upon it for **ferreting** out and arresting the **perpetrators** of these outrages. Gangs of outlaws, styling themselves "Regulators," were formed in some of the State districts, who committed these outrages not only upon the persons of freed people, but upon loyal white citizens, whose houses were often burned, and they themselves driven from their homes. It has been reported at these headquarters by officers of the bureau that these . . . regulators offered to kill any freedmen who refused to contract with the planters for a fixed sum per head. The civil authorities were powerless to act, had they had the will to do so; the military were sent out, but could accomplish little, there being no cavalry in the State, as the outlaws were mounted. The inhabitants would give no information against them, whether from fear of their vengeance or because of **collusion** with them I am unable to judge . . .

The aged and **infirm** freedmen were turned off by their former owners, in whose service they had spent their strength, to shift for themselves, and had not this bureau extended aid to them, very many would inevitably have perished on the highways. Camps and hospitals were established, and large numbers of wretched victims of slavery were gathered together and fed and clothed by the bureau. Many white persons, suffering extreme poverty, were also supplied with food and clothing. On issuing days might be seen

The Union in Crisis   Primary Source

the white lady of respectability standing side by side with the African, both awaiting their turn to receive their weekly supply of rations . . .

The schools for freed people in this State are in successful operation, under the supervision of Mr. R. Tomlinson, who by his energy and zeal has done much to establish them on a permanent basis. There is a strong desire on the part of this race of people to obtain the knowledge which was denied to them while in the bonds of slavery; their progress is very creditable to them, and their examinations would not be discreditable to a school of white children under the same circumstances. Much opposition is thrown in the way of establishing schools for their education by the citizens in some of the districts of the State, who seem determined to keep these poor people as ignorant as they were when slaves; but in some of the other districts the people feel the necessity for the education of this class of people. The teachers from the north are denied board in all southern families, yet I am happy to say that, with a few exceptions, they are among the most self-denying, laborious and useful members among the different agencies of the bureau. It is interesting to see the **avidity** with which the freed children avail themselves of the means of instruction offered them. There are thirty-eight schools established, employing 91 teachers, and they have an attendance of 5,465 scholars.

Source: U.S. Senate 39th Congress, 2nd Session, Senate Executive Document No. 6, 1866

WHAT DID YOU LEARN?

1. According to this source how did the former slave-owners in South Carolina treat the recently freed African Americans? Why do you think they treated them this way?

____

____

2. Who were the "Regulators"? Why was it so difficult to stop them?

____

____

3. What were the accomplishments of the Freedmen's Bureau in South Carolina?

____

____

History and Geography

The South Secedes

Many people believed the presidential election of 1860 would determine the future of slavery in the United States. When Abraham Lincoln was elected in November 1860, secessionists immediately began calling for withdrawal from the Union. By the time Lincoln became president in March 1861, a number of states had already seceded from the Union. States continued to secede even after the fighting between North and South began.

Use the table below and the map on the following page to complete the Map Activity and answer the questions that follow.

Secession of Southern States, 1860–1861	
State	**Date Seceded**
Alabama	January 11, 1861
Arkansas	May 6, 1861
Florida	January 10, 1861
Georgia	January 19, 1861
Louisiana	January 26, 1861
Mississippi	January 5, 1861
North Carolina	May 21, 1861
South Carolina	December 1860
Tennessee	May 7, 1861
Texas	February 23, 1861
Virginia	May 23, 1861

MAP ACTIVITY

1. Using a highlighter or colored pen, shade the states that seceded before March 1861. Use the same color to fill in the appropriate box in the map's key.

2. Using a different color, shade the states that seceded after March 1861 and through May 1861 and fill in the corresponding box in the map's key.

3. Write a number in each state indicating the order in which the states seceded, "1" being first.

The Union in Crisis   # History and Geography

The South Secedes

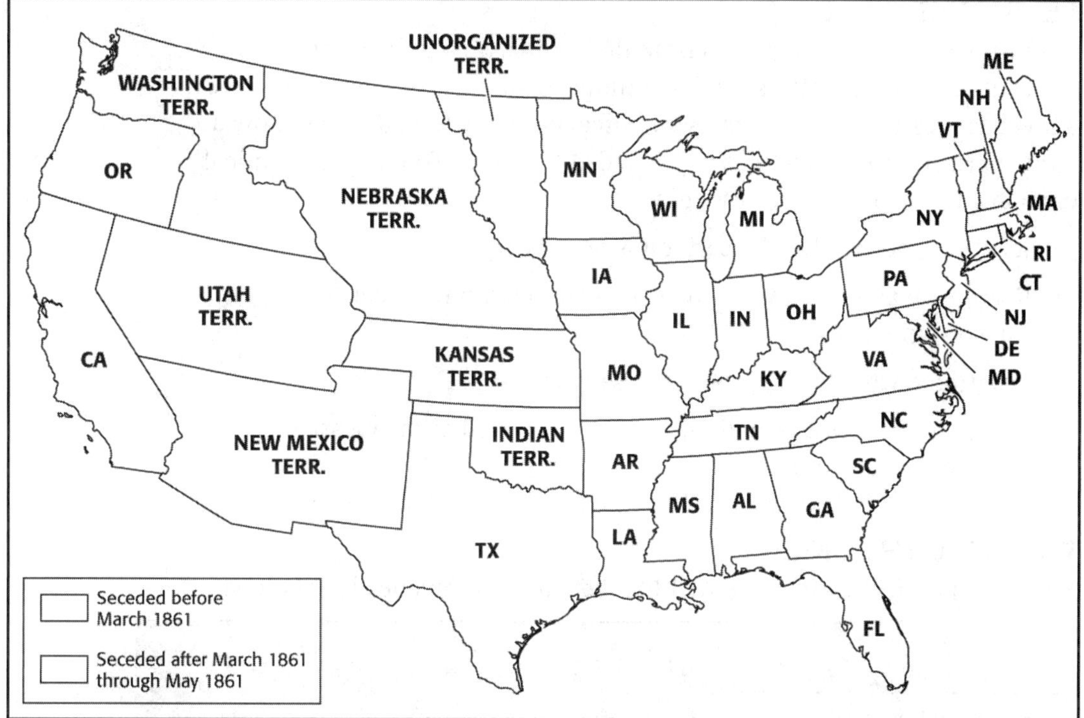

ANALYZING MAPS

1. **Analyze** Which was the first state to secede?

____

2. **Analyze** Abraham Lincoln was elected in November 1860 but did not take office until March 1861. List the states that seceded before Lincoln took office.

____

3. **Region** Missouri, Kentucky, Maryland, and Delaware were also slave states. Did they secede? Based on what you have learned in your studies, what was this group of states called at the time?

____

4. **Analyze** The Civil War began with the Confederate attack on Fort Sumter on April 12, 1861. Which states seceded after the attack on Fort Sumter?

____

EXTENSION ACTIVITY

Slavery was a major issue that led to the secession of the South from the Union. Was it the only issue? Research to determine whether other issues also helped lead to secession. Write a short essay about your findings.

The Union in Crisis   Social Studies Skills

Interpreting Political Cartoons

LEARN THE SKILL

Political cartoons are a type of visual that expresses a point of view. In political cartoons, artists use exaggerations of subjects or events to convey a specific message. Historians use political cartoons to understand how a particular person or event was perceived at the time. To interpret political cartoons, try the following strategies.

- Identify who or what the cartoon is portraying.

- Read the text and study all the symbols, looking for clues to the cartoon's point of view.

- Determine what the cartoon's message is.

- Compare the message with the facts—ask whether the message is historically accurate.

PRACTICE THE SKILL

Study the political cartoon from 1860, then answer the questions below.

APPLY THE SKILL

1. Who or what is the cartoon portraying?

____

2. What is the artist's message? What clues lead you to that message?

____

3. Do you think this cartoon was drawn by a Lincoln supporter or opponent? Why?

____

John Brown's Raid

This essay assignment will help you practice for the writing portion of the SAT. You will be asked to write a short essay in which you develop a point of view on a given topic using appropriate reasons and examples. You will be given 25 minutes to write this essay. Follow the steps below to help you use the time wisely and give you practice in writing short essays.

THINK ABOUT THE FOLLOWING ISSUE

John Brown's capture of the federal arsenal at Harpers Ferry, Virginia, electrified the nation. Many southerners viewed Brown's actions as an act of terrorism that revealed how far northerners would go to end slavery. Many northerners saw Brown's attack as a violent but necessary step in the process of ending slavery.

ASSIGNMENT

Was Brown's attack an act of terrorism, or a reasonable attempt to end slavery? Write a short essay in which you develop your position on this issue. Support your point of view with reasoning and examples from your reading and studies.

Prewriting (2–3 minutes)

1. Remember that the writing portion of the SAT is a timed assignment. You will have only 25 minutes to write the essay, but spending 2 or 3 minutes on these prewriting tasks will allow you to organize your thoughts and will help you write your essay.

2. Think about the issue and decide on your point of view.

3. Think about what the main ideas of your essay will be. What details will you use to support those ideas?

4. Prepare a short outline to organize your thoughts. Remember that your essay will need an organized, coherent structure in order to do well on the SAT.

Writing (20 minutes)

1. Your essay should be carefully structured and written in paragraph form. You should have three parts to your essay: an introduction, which presents your thesis and main ideas; a body, which elaborates on your ideas and supports those ideas with details; and a conclusion, which sums up your essay.

2. It is important to show that you can effectively develop your ideas. Present your point of view logically and clearly. Stay focused on your topic.

3. You will have only 25 minutes to write your essay, so use your time wisely.

The Union in Crisis

Writing for the SAT

Proofreading (2-3 minutes)

1. Try to leave a few minutes to reread your essay and make revisions.

2. Last, check the following:

   • Capitalization and spelling of all proper names and places

   • Punctuation, grammar, and spelling

EVALUATING

SAT essays are graded on a scale of 1 to 6, with 6 being the highest score. The maker of the SAT, the College Board, describes the grading system as follows:

• **Score of 6:** An essay in this category effectively and insightfully develops a point of view on the issue and demonstrates outstanding critical thinking. It is well organized, clearly focused, and free of most errors in grammar, usage, and mechanics.

• **Score of 5:** An essay in this category effectively develops a point of view on the issue and demonstrates strong critical thinking. It is well organized and focused, and is generally free of most errors in grammar, usage and mechanics.

• **Score of 4:** An essay in this category develops a point of view on the issue and demonstrates competent critical thinking. It is generally organized and focused, and has some errors in grammar, usage, and mechanics.

• **Score of 3:** An essay in this category develops a point of view on the issue, but may do so inconsistently or use inadequate evidence to support its position. It is limited in its organization or focus, and contains an accumulation of errors in grammar, usage, and mechanics.

• **Score of 2:** An essay in this category develops a point of view on the issue that is vague or seriously limited and provides inappropriate or insufficient evidence to support its position. It is poorly organized, and contains errors so serious that meaning is somewhat obscured.

• **Score of 1:** An essay in this category develops no viable point of view on the issue, or provides little or no evidence to support its position. It is disorganized or unfocused, and contains pervasive errors in grammar, usage, or mechanics that persistently interfere with meaning.

• **Score of 0:** Essays not on the assignment will receive a score of zero.

The Union in Crisis

Chapter Review

MAIN IDEAS

1. By 1850 the issue of slavery dominated national politics, leading to sectional divisions and, finally, the secession of the southern states.
2. The Civil War broke out following a Confederate attack on Fort Sumter, leading to widespread fighting, heavy casualties, and the eventual defeat of the Confederacy.
3. Conflicting plans for dealing with the post-Civil War South had long-lasting effects on government and the economy.

REVIEWING VOCABULARY, TERMS, AND PEOPLE

In the space provided, write the vocabulary term that best matches each description.

_____________________ 1. The act that decided that popular sovereignty would settle the issue of slavery in Kansas Territory

_____________________ 2. The law that made it a federal crime to aid runaway slaves and allowed the arrest of escaped slaves

_____________________ 3. The first major battle of the Civil War

_____________________ 4. Three-day battle in Pennsylvania that left 28,000 Confederate soldiers and 23,000 northern soldiers dead

_____________________ 5. The document that freed slaves in states that were rebelling against the United States

_____________________ 6. Amendment that ended slavery in the United States

_____________________ 7. The period of time during which the United States made policies to rebuilt the South following the Civil War

_____________________ 8. The name that ex-Confederates gave to those southerners who supported Reconstruction

_____________________ 9. The act that gave citizenship to African Americans and guaranteed them the same legal rights as white Americans

_____________________ 10. A group that formed to maintain white control over the South

The Union in Crisis   Chapter Review

COMPREHENSION AND CRITICAL THINKING

Answer the questions on the lines provided.

1. Why did some states secede after the election of 1860?

   ____

   ____

2. What was a new type of labor system that arose in the South following the Civil War, and how did it work?

   ____

   ____

3. What were some reasons that Reconstruction ended?

   ____

   ____

REVIEWING THEMES

In the space provided, explain how each term relates to the theme listed below.

Theme: geography

1. Compromise of 1850 ____

   ____

2. Emancipation Proclamation ____

   ____

3. carpetbaggers ____

   ____

Vocabulary Builder

SECTION 1

1. a
2. d
3. a
4. b
5. Answer should be a complete sentence that includes the term *Compromise of 1850*.
6. Answer should be a complete sentence that includes the term *Confederate States of America* and explains that its constitution specifically recognized slavery and guaranteed the rights of citizens to own slaves.
7. Answer should be a complete sentence that includes the term *Kansas-Nebraska Act* and explains that Lincoln returned to politics.

SECTION 2

1. Battle of Gettysburg
2. Emancipation Proclamation
3. Battle of Bull Run
4. Battle of Chancellorsville
5. Battle of Antietam
6. Thirteenth Amendment
7. Battle of Shiloh

Answers will vary, but should be a letter that relates to the section and includes at least five of the following terms: *Battle of Antietam, Battle of Bull Run, Battle of Chancellorsville, Battle of Gettysburg, Battle of Shiloh, Emancipation Proclamation, Fort Sumter, Thirteenth Amendment.*

SECTION 3

Answers will vary, but should be a summary of what students learned in the section that includes at least five of the following terms: *carpetbagger, Civil Rights Act of 1866, contract, Fifteenth Amendment, Fourteenth Amendment, Ku Klux Klan, Liberal Republicans, prejudice, Reconstruction, scalawag, sharecropping, tenant farming, utilize.*

1. Fourteenth Amendment
2. Ku Klux Klan
3. carpetbaggers
4. sharecropping
5. Fifteenth Amendment
6. Liberal Republicans

Biography

Harriet Beecher Stowe

WHAT DID YOU LEARN?

1. Her father was a prominent Congregationalist minister.
2. Answers will vary. The book came to stand for many things. Because it exposed the evils of slavery, it came to symbolize the antislavery movement. It came to symbolize the differences between North and South, and it came to be seen as a voice for the oppressed.

ACTIVITY

Students should work in groups of five or six to select a passage from the stage version of the book or from the book itself. Groups should re-enact the scene for the class. When all the scenes have been presented, discuss students' reactions to the story. Draw parallels between the themes of the book and some of the social issues faced in the United States today.

Stonewall Jackson

WHAT DID YOU LEARN?

1. Jackson could hold a position against enemy assault and maneuver his troops around enemy lines to make surprise attacks. He was a strong leader and won many battles.
2. Answers will vary. Students should support the words they suggest. Students might select the word *hero* and then cite the battles he participated in.

ACTIVITY

Students should work together to map out one of Jackson's battles. Maps should include a description of the battle and Jackson's military strategies. As maps are presented to the class, discuss the elements of Jackson's strategies.

Sojourner Truth
WHAT DID YOU LEARN?

1. She helped gather supplies for the African American regiments. She also was an outspoken advocate for ending slavery.
2. She believed she had been called by the Holy Spirit to spread the word of God.

ACTIVITY

Answers will vary. Sojourner Truth stood for many things, including individual rights and God-given freedoms. Students' writing should reflect an understanding of her life and beliefs, as well as the results of her work.

Literature
Shiloh
ANALYZING LITERATURE

1. Student answers should use details from the excerpt to support their descriptions of General Johnston. For example, they may describe him as a leader of his men (citing his getting the men back in line by riding the line and touching his cup to the points of their bayonets, followed by his cry of "I will lead you!"), and one who enjoyed the battle, with his "eyes that had a shine like bright glass" and his laughter after his battle injuries. He showed care for all men, as illustrated by his sending his surgeon to take care of the wounded prisoners.
2. Palmer's father may have been referring to the idealism of fighting and dying for a cause, and how this can reflect the values of honor, generosity, and valor. General Johnston leading the soldiers into battle, the men charging through the thick fire to take the crest of the hill, and Johnston's asking his doctor to take care of the prisoners reflects these values, but in the end these actions also bring death, which may be the point of Palmer's father using the term "misplaced" chivalry.

Primary Source
Southern and Northern Reactions to the Civil War
WHAT DID YOU LEARN?
Mary Boykin Chestnut

1. Chesnut dreaded the outbreak of war. She feared that war would bring invasion from Yankee soldiers and insurrection from the slaves. It is likely Chesnut was also fearful for her husband's safety.

Mary Ashton Livermore

1. Large numbers of men left their jobs to enlist in the military. People flew flags nearly everywhere in support of the war effort. Concerns about the war caused people to forget about their daily routines.

MAKE A COMPARISON

1. Southerners and northerners responded differently. Northerners were eager to fight, some to end slavery and others to preserve the Union. Southerners faced divided loyalties. Some southern states remained loyal to the Union yet refused to provide troops to fight against fellow Southerners. The Confederacy responded to the war with anger and defiance.
2. The two passages differ in tone. Chesnut's description is largely somber, containing her own anguished reactions. Livermore's passage is upbeat and optimistic. The passages differ because of when they were written. Chesnut's diary entry was written at the time the described events happened. She thus recorded her fears about the upcoming war. Livermore wrote her passage after the war had ended. The Northern victory allowed her to be upbeat in her descriptions.

Report of the South Carolina Freedmen's Bureau
WHAT DID YOU LEARN?

1. Former slave-owners in South Carolina treated the newly-freed African Americans harshly. They tortured the freedmen and

forced them to work on their plantations. Old and sick freedmen were cast off the plantations, left to fend for themselves. The former slave-owners did this because they considered African Americans to be inferior and they were angry about the end of slavery.

2. Regulators were bands of outlaws who terrorized African Americans and any whites who tried to help them. They were difficult to stop because they were mounted and there were no cavalry units in South Carolina. Also, people were afraid to help authorities capture the regulators.

3. The Freedmen's Bureau supplied food, clothing, and medical aid to the sick and impoverished. Both white and black people received this help from the Bureau. The Freedmen's Bureau also set up schools in the state for African Americans.

History and Geography
The South Secedes
MAP ACTIVITY

1. Students should shade the following states, and the box next to "Seceded before March 1861," with one color: Alabama, Florida, Georgia, Louisiana, Mississippi, South Carolina, and Texas.

2. Students should shade the following states, and the box next to "Seceded after March and through May 1861," in a second color: Arkansas, North Carolina, Tennessee, and Virginia.

3. States should be numbered in the following order: 1–South Carolina; 2–Mississippi; 3–Florida; 4–Alabama; 5–Georgia; 6–Louisiana; 7–Texas; 8–Arkansas; 9–Tennessee; 10–North Carolina; 11–Virginia.

ANALYZING MAPS

1. South Carolina
2. Alabama, Florida, Georgia, Louisiana, Mississippi, South Carolina, and Texas
3. no; border states

4. Arkansas, North Carolina, Tennessee, and Virginia

EXTENSION ACTIVITY
Student answers will vary, but should show they have researched the causes of the Civil War. Students may report on political, social, and economic issues that also increased tensions between North and South.

Social Studies Skills
Interpreting Political Cartoons
APPLY THE SKILL

1. The cartoon portrays the election of 1860 as a footrace between Abraham Lincoln, John Bell, John C. Breckinridge, and Stephen Douglas.

2. The message is that Lincoln will easily win the political race for the presidency in 1860. Clues: Lincoln is depicted much larger than the others and is leaping effortlessly over them. The other candidates look frustrated or angry.

3. This cartoon was most likely drawn by a Lincoln supporter who wanted to show Lincoln as the superior candidate in the race.

Writing for the SAT
John Brown's Raid
Student essays should be evaluated using the scoring rubric provided in the activity.

Chapter Review
REVIEWING VOCABULARY, TERMS, AND PEOPLE

1. Kansas-Nebraska Act
2. Fugitive Slave Act
3. Battle of Bull Run
4. Battle of Gettysburg
5. Emancipation Proclamation
6. Thirteenth Amendment
7. Reconstruction
8. scalawags
9. Civil Rights Act of 1866
10. Ku Klux Klan

COMPREHENSION AND CRITICAL THINKING

1. Some southern states seceded after the election of 1860 because both houses of Congress were in northern hands and because the newly elected president, Abraham Lincoln, opposed slavery.
2. In sharecropping, workers would receive a share of their employer's crop for their agricultural labor, instead of earning wages.
3. Reconstruction ended for many reasons. The following are sample answers. Reconstruction ended because its fiercest leaders died; a depression captured the attention of Republican leaders; Supreme Court decisions weakened protections of Reconstruction; President Grant refused to help state leaders who were under assault by southern Democratic leaders and by their supporters; Republicans compromised the 1876 election by agreeing to withdraw remaining federal troops from the South.

REVIEWING THEMES

1. All provisions of the Compromise of 1850 related to geography. The provisions were the following: admitting California to the Union as a free state; setting the New Mexico-Texas border; organizing the New Mexico and Utah territories, with slavery in each to be decided by popular sovereignty; the Fugitive Slave Act; outlawing the buying and selling of slaves in Washington, D.C.
2. The Emancipation Proclamation freed all slaves in areas that were rebelling against the United States.
3. A carpetbagger was a northerner who came to the South to take part in its reconstruction.